Marilyn Monroe:
Quotes & Facts

By Blago Kirov

First Edition

*****

Marilyn Monroe: Quotes & Facts

*****

Table of Contents

Foreword

"I'm very definitely a woman and I enjoy it."

This book is an anthology of Quotes from Marilyn Monroe and Facts about Marilyn Monroe. It grants her reflections on subjects ranging from Sex and Love to Art and Life; in addition, the book shows the personality of Marilyn Monroe into a different light.

Marilyn Monroe was born June 1, 1926, in Los Angeles, California, as Norma Jeane Mortenson, church-registered baptismal name Norma Jeane Baker. She died August 5, 1962, in Brentwood, Los Angeles. Marilyn was an American film actress and singer, model and film producer. She became a world star in the 1950s and is now a film icon regarded as the archetypal sex-symbol of the 20th century.

Marilyn Monroe grew up as a half-orphan with foster parents and temporarily in an orphanage. She was discovered as a model in 1944 and photographed in the course of her life by the most renowned photographers of her time. In 1946 she got a contract as a young actress. Marilyn played her first leading role in the B-movie Ladies of the Chorus (1948). In the movie noir The Asphalt Jungle (1950), she could show her acting talent for the first time. Although she only played small supporting roles as an attractive blonde in many early movies, she became the darling of the audience and a guarantor of success for the studios.

Marilyn Monroe was at her time the most famous and most photographed woman in the world. Despite her success and many awards, she suffered from being perceived as a curvaceous beauty and not as a serious actress. Her three marriages failed, and also her fervent wish for children remained unfulfilled. In her last years, she also had to struggle with psychological problems and her addiction to tablets. She couldn't ever feel wholly free herself from her image of the attractive, inexperienced blonde. It was only after her death that this image was revised and her artistic work recognized and honored. In 1999 she was ranked sixth among the most celebrated female American film stars by the American Film Institute.

"Dogs never bite me. Just humans."

Her Words

"A nice lady even though she turned down making a picture with me. That just shows how smart she is." (About Mae West)

"An actress is not a machine, but they treat you like a machine. A money machine "

"Arthur did this to me. He could have written anything and he comes up with this. If that's what he thinks of me, well, then I'm not for him and he's not for me. Arthur says it's his movie. I don't think he even wants me in it." (About Arthur Miller's script for 'The Misfits')

"Do not presume to have been the first in my heart, if you were not smart enough to be the last."

"Grace McKee arranged the marriage for me, I never had a choice. There's not much to say about it. They couldn't support me, and they had to work out something. And so I got married."

"He is a man at the top of his profession and is a fine actor as well. You know, he got an Oscar for From Here to Eternity (1953). He has helped more people anonymously than anybody else. And the miserable press smears him with lies about his being involved with the Mafia and gangsters. And Frank just takes it." (About Frank Sinatra)

"Here is Joyce writing what a woman thinks to herself. Can he, does he really know her innermost thoughts? But after I read the whole book, I could better understand that Joyce is an artist who could penetrate the souls of people, male or female. It really doesn't matter that Joyce doesn't have...or never felt a menstrual cramp. To me Leopold Bloom is a central character. He is the despised Irish Jew, married to an Irish Catholic woman. It is through them Joyce develops much of what he wants to say. Do you agree that the scene where Bloom is looking at the little girl on the swing is the most erotic in the book?" (About James Joyce and the character of Molly Bloom in Ulysses)

"He's the only person I know that is in worse shape than I am." (About Montgomery Clift)

"I am invariably late for appointments--sometimes as much as two hours. I've tried to change my ways but the things that make me late are too strong."

"I believe in everything a little, and if I have kids, I think they should be Jewish. Anyway, I can identify with the Jews. Everybody's out to get them no matter what they do." (About why she converted to Judaism)

"I read his "Introductory Lectures," God, what a genius. He makes it so understandable. And he is so right. Didn't he say himself that (William Shakespeare) and (Fyodor Dostoevsky) had a better understanding of psychology than all the scientists put together? Damn it, they do." (About Sigmund Freud)

"I want to have your child. With my looks and your brains, it will be a perfect child!" (In conversation with Albert Einstein)

"I was surprised to be so crazy about Joe. I expected a flashy New York sports type, and instead I met this reserved guy who didn't make a pass at me right away! He treated me like something special. Joe is a very decent man, and he makes other people feel decent, too." (About meeting Joe DiMaggio for the first time)

"I'm not going to the beach to get dark, I like being blonde."

"Imperfection is beauty, madness is genius and it's better to be absolutely ridiculous than absolutely boring."

"It would be so nice to have a president who looks so young and good-looking." (About John F. Kennedy)

"Jean Harlow was my idol." (About her favorite actress)

"Johann Wolfgang Goethe said, "Talent is developed in privacy", you know? And it's really true. There is a need for aloneness which I don't think most people realize for an actor. It's almost having certain kinds of secrets for yourself that you'll let the whole world in on only for a moment, when you're acting."

"Laugh when you're sad, mourn is too easy."

"My marriage didn't make me sad, but it didn't make me happy either. My husband and I hardly spoke to each other. This wasn't because we were angry. We had nothing to say. I was dying of boredom." (About why she divorced James Dougherty)

"My sin has been no more than I have written, posing for the nude because I desperately needed 50 dollars to get my car out of hock." (on her famous nude calendar pose in 1949)

"People started saying I was a lesbian. I smiled. There is no wrong sex if there is love in it."

"The man has to stimulate the mind and spirit of women to make sex interesting. The real lover is the man who thrills to touch his head, smile or her eyes. "

"The world around me then was kind of grim. I had to learn to pretend in order to - I don't know - block the grimness. The whole world seemed sort of closed to me . . . (I felt) on the outside of everything, and all I could do was to dream up any kind of pretend game." (About drifting in and out of orphanages when she was little)
 (About her early marriage to James Dougherty)

"A career is born in public - talent in privacy."

"A career is wonderful, but you can't curl up with it on a cold night."

"A friend tells you what you want to hear; a best friend tells you the truth."

"A girl doesn't need anyone who doesn't need her"

"A sex symbol becomes a thing. I hate being a thing."

"A wise girl kisses but doesn't love, listens but doesn't believe, and leaves before she is left."

"A wise girl knows her limits; a smart girl knows that she has none."

"A woman can't be alone. She needs a man. A man and a woman support and strengthen each other. She just can't do it by herself. "

"All a girl really wants is for one guy to prove to her that they are not all the same."

"All girls are beautiful in their own way"

"All little girls should be told they are pretty, even if they aren't."

"Always, always, always believe in yourself, because if you don't, then who will, Sweetie? So keep your head high, keep your chin up, and most importantly, keep smiling, because life's a beautiful thing and there's so much to smile about."

"Before marriage, a girl has to make love to a man to hold him. After marriage, she has to hold him to make love to him."

"Being a sex symbol is a heavy load to carry, especially when one is tired, hurt and bewildered."

"Beneath the makeup and behind the smile I am just a girl who wishes for the world."

"But if you can't handle me at my worst, then you sure as hell don't deserve me at my best. ..."

"Disappointments make you open your eyes and close your heart."

"Dogs never bite me. Just humans."

"Dreaming about being an actress, is more exciting then being one."

"Ever notice how 'What the hell' is always the right answer?"

"Everyone's a star and deserves the right to twinkle."

"Fame is fickle and I know it. It has its compensations, but it also has its drawbacks and I've experienced them both."

"First, I'm trying to prove to myself that I'm a person. Then maybe I'll convince myself that I'm an actress. "

"Hollywood is a place where they'll pay you a thousand dollars for a kiss and fifty cents for your soul."

"Hopefully the wait will not wear my dreams."

"How wrong it is for a woman to expect the man to build the world she wants, rather than to create it herself."

"Husbands are chiefly good as lovers when they are betraying their wives."

"I am no jealousy; I have fear that someone else discover how amazing you are."

"I believe that everything happens for a reason. People change so that you can learn to let go, things go wrong so that you appreciate them when they're right, you believe lies so you eventually learn to trust no one but yourself, and sometimes good things fall apart so better things can fall together."

"I do sin, but I am not the devil. I am just a small girl in a big world trying to find someone to love."

"I don't know who invented high heels, but all women owe him a lot!"

"I don't mind being burdened with being glamorous and sexual. Beauty and femininity are ageless and can't be contrived, and glamour, although the manufacturers won't like this, cannot be manufactured. Not real glamour; it's based on femininity."

"I don't mind living in a man's world, as long as I can be a woman in it."

"I don't mind making jokes, but I don't want to look like one."

"I don't understand why people aren't a little more generous with each other."

"I don't want to make money; I just want to be wonderful."

"I have feelings too. I am still human. All I want is to be loved, for myself and for my talent. "

"I have too many fantasies to be a housewife.... I guess I am a fantasy."
"I just want to be wonderful."

"I knew I belonged to the public and to the world, not because I was talented or even beautiful, but because I had never belonged to anything or anyone else."

"I like to be fully dressed, or if not, totally naked. I do not like half-measures. "

"I restore myself when I'm alone."

"If I'd observed all the rules I'd never have got anywhere."

"If I'm a star, then the people made me a star."

"I'm selfish, impatient and a little insecure. I make mistakes, I am out of control and at times hard to handle. But if you can't handle me at my worst, then you sure as hell don't deserve me at my best."

"I'm trying to find myself as a person, sometimes that's not easy to do. Millions of people live their entire lives without finding themselves. But it is something I must do. The best way for me to find myself as a person is to prove to myself that I am an actress."

"I'm trying to find myself as a person, sometimes that's not easy to do. Millions of people live their entire lives without finding themselves. But it is something I must do. The best way for me to find myself as a person is to prove to myself that I am an actress."

"I'm very definitely a woman and I enjoy it."

"In Hollywood a girl's virtue is much less important than her hair-do.

"It stirs up envy, fame does. People feel fame gives them some kind of privilege to walk up to you and say anything to you - and it won't hurt your feelings - like it's happening to your clothing."

"It's better to be unhappy alone than unhappy with someone."

"It's not true that I had nothing on. I had the radio on." (Answer on her nude in Playboy magazine)

"It's often just enough to be with someone. I don't need to touch them. Not even talk. A feeling passes between you both. You're not alone."

"I've been on a calendar, but I've never been on time."

"I've never dropped anyone I believed in."

"I've never liked the name Marilyn. I've often wished that I had held out that day for Jean Monroe. But I guess it's to do anything about it."

"Life is too beautiful to wake up with worries, spend the day with anger, and go to sleep sadly."

"Living alone is like being at a party where nobody pays you attention. "

"Love doesn't need to be perfect it just needs to be true."

"Men are always ready to respect anything that bores them."

"No sex is wrong if there is love in it."

"Sex is part of nature. I go along with nature."

"Success makes so many people hate you. I wish it was not that way. It would be wonderful to enjoy success without seeing envy in the eyes of those around you."

"The body is meant to be seen, not all covered up."

"The friendship ends where mistrust begins."

"The thing I want more than anything else? I want to have children. I used to feel for every child I had, I would adopt another."

"The trouble with censors is that they worry if a girl has cleavage. They ought to worry if she hasn't any."

"The women's best friends are diamonds."

"True happiness comes from within, not from anyone else."

"What do I wear in bed? Why, Chanel No. 5, of course"

"What good is it being Marilyn Monroe? Why I can not just be an ordinary woman? A woman can have a family ... I'd settle for a single baby. My own baby."

"You do not know why children fight and then they will play together? Because your happiness is worth more than your pride."

"You know who I always depend on? Not strangers, not friends. The telephone! That's my best friend. I seldom write letters, but I love calling friends, especially late at night, when I can't sleep."

"Your clothes should be tight enough to show you're a woman but loose enough to show you're a lady".

Dates and Facts

Childhood and youth

Marilyn Monroe was the unwanted child of film editor Gladys Pearl Baker, née Monroe (1902-1984). Her father was probably Charles Stanley Gifford, but other admirers of Gladys are also possible.

Gifford was Gladys' supervisor in the editing studio of RKO Pictures. She had an affair with him in 1925. When he found out about the pregnancy of his lover, he left her.

Although he had never confessed to his daughter, Marilyn Monroe was convinced throughout her life that Charles Gifford was her father.

Gladys was married to the honorary reader Martin Edward Mortensen at the time of birth but had been separated from him for a long time.

With her first husband, John Baker she had two children, Robert "Jack" Kermit, and Berniece Inez Gladys, who had lived with her father since the divorce.

Marilyn Monroe was born Norma Jeane Mortenson at the General Hospital in Los Angeles on June 1, 1926.

Gladys' father was Edward Mortenson, a baker with an unknown address.

At the church baptism on December 6, 1926, Gladys'
mother Della Mae Monroe, née Hogan, registered the
name Norma Jeane Baker, the surname of Gladys' first
husband. With this, the grandmother tried to cover up
the illegitimacy of the child.

In many biographies, Norma Jeane's middle name is
written without "e" at the end.

Twelve days after the birth, the working mother gave
her child to the strictly religious Pentecostals Ida and
Albert Wayne Bolender in Hawthorne for a small fee.
Ida and Wayne Bolender had a son and repeatedly took
in foster children.

The first seven years of her life Norma Jeane grew up
well protected. At first, she called Ida and Albert
"Mommy" and "Daddy" and did not know that the red-
haired lady she visited from time to time was her
mother.

She was raised very religiously, went to church
regularly and was inseparable from the boy of the same
age, Lester.

In 1933, when she was seven years old, a neighbor shot
her beloved dog, Tippy. The sensitive girl did not get
over this loss, and the Bolenders had to call her mother
for help. In the meantime, Gladys had saved enough
money for a bungalow and took her daughter back.

A little later, however, triggered by the suicide of her grandfather Tilford Marion Hogan, Gladys suffered a nervous breakdown and fell mentally ill. In 1934 she was admitted to Los Angeles General Hospital, later transferred to the State Hospital in Norwalk.

Norma Jeane became a social orphan. The following time she spent with different foster parents. Finally, Grace McKee, her mother's best friend, took care of her.

"Tante Grace," who loved movies, took Norma Jeane to the movies regularly and aroused her enthusiasm for the movie.

At the beginning of 1935, she married the sales representative Ervin "Doc" Goddard". Grace had to give Norma Jeane to the orphanage of Los Angeles for 22 months for financial reasons but continued to take care of her. Although Norma Jeane was cared for in this house, the orphanage remained in her traumatic memory for the rest of her life.

In 1936 Grace received guardianship over Norma Jeane and brought her back in 1937. After her foster father Goddard, drunk and was insistent with the girl, Grace gave her to Ida Martin, a distant relative of Norma Jeane.

Shortly before her twelfth birthday, her thirteen-year-old cousin "forced" her to sexual acts, which must have been physically and emotionally painful for her.

Finally, in 1938, Grace gave her to her aunt. Ana Lower, who also lived in Van Nuys, was a relatively wealthy, warm-hearted widow of mature age. With "Aunt Ana," she found support and trust. Later she said that Ana was "the only person who let me know what love means."

From September 1939 Norma Jeane attended Emerson Junior High School in Westwood Village. Her performance was average in most subjects, and she showed talent in journalism. She wrote humorous texts for the school newspaper, including an essay that stated that men prefer blondes.

As a young girl, she had been very shy. When she was supposed to speak to her classmates, she began to stutter.

At the age of 13, she had grown into a beauty who was courted by the boys of her school.

As Ana Lower became older, she was increasingly struggling with serious health problems, and Norma Jeane lived with the Goddards for some time.

She had found a good friend in her peer Eleanor "Bebe" Goddard, with whom she attended Van Nuys High School from September 1941.

In 1942, "Doc" Goddard decided to move to West Virginia with Grace and Bebe for professional reasons. Norma Jeane was not to accompany them.

In the meantime, she had made friends with James "Jim" Dougherty, who was five years older from the neighbors. Since neither Grace Goddard nor Ana Lower could take care of her any longer, Grace arranged the marriage of the young couple with Jim's mother.

On June 19, 1942, two and a half weeks after her sixteenth birthday, Norma Jeane married her boyfriend and was thus saved from having to return to an orphanage or to foster parents. However, the laws governing married under-age children forced her to leave the University High School in West Los Angeles, which she had recently attended. This denied her a school leaving certificate.

Model and small film rolls 1945-1947

In 1944 Norma Jeane Dougherty worked in the assembly department of an armaments factory, where she painted aircraft models. In the fall of that year, an army photographer from the First Motion Picture Unit, known as the "Celluloid Command," discovered her as a model at her workplace. David Conover had been commissioned by the then captain and later U.S. president Ronald Reagan to "make animated pictures of attractive women on the assembly line who support the war effort through their work" Such pictures had already achieved cult status under the title Rosie the Riveter. The first photos appeared in the U.S. Army's Yank magazine in mid-1945.

Conover recognized her talent and advised her to apply as a model.

In June 1945 Emmeline Snively of The Blue Book Agency in Hollywood offered her a contract. There she also trained as a model and mannequin.

She discussed all her photographs with the photographers and always worked on perfecting her expression.

On the agency's advice, she had her brunettes and curly hair blonde and smoothed for a shampoo advertisement for the first time.

One of her first photographers was André de Dienes. The young Norma Jeane joined him on a photo tour through California, Nevada, and Washington.

She quickly established herself as one of the agency's most popular models. As early as 1946 she first appeared on the cover of a national magazine.

From 1947 she appeared on the front pages of numerous magazines worldwide.

At the instigation of her new agent Helen Ainsworth,
Norma Jeane had an interview with Ben Lyon, the 20th
Century Fox talent finder.

On July 19, 1946, she made her first film tests. Lyon had required four of the best people of the "Fox." With the approval of vice president and production manager Darryl F. Zanuck, she got a half-year contract as a young actress shortly afterward.

The employment contract, which was later extended by six months with double payments, was rewarded with 75 dollars per week, regardless of whether she worked or not.

Together with Ben Lyon, she chose an artist's name. Although her "Marilyn," after the dancer Marilyn Miller, did not appeal to her at first, she let Lyon convince her. As of the last name she chose the birth name of her mother.

She was in the studio every day, taking classes in singing and dancing and trying to learn as much as she could.

Her first engagement was in 1947 as an extra in the musical comedy The Shocking Miss Pilgrim.

She made her debut in the comedy Scudda Hoo! Scudda Hay!, which was first released in 1948. In a scene of a few seconds after going to church, she greets the protagonist, played by June Haver, with "Hi, Rad!", who then greets her back with "Hi, Betty! All other scenes in which she can be seen while canoeing was cut out.

Besides another extra's role in You Were Meant for Me, she had a small role as waitress Evie in the film Dangerous Years. Both movies were neither Marilyn Monroe's career favorable nor success for the studio. Therefore the contract after one year was not extended.

Already in January 1947, the studio had sent some of the young actors to the Actors Laboratory for further education. Here she continued to work, had contact with experienced theater actors from New York, studied theater scenes, got to know social and political topics and serious acting.

The growing popularity and first central role 1948-1952

In March 1948, Marilyn Monroe signed a six-month contract with Columbia Pictures through Joe Schenks, Chairman of the Fox Board of Directors.

Studio boss Harry Cohn required that she bleached her hair and had the fine hairline removed by electrolysis.

In the same year, she took acting lessons with Natascha Lytess, the acting teacher at Columbia.

Lytess stood up for her, and in the summer of that year, Monroe made her first big appearance in the musical adaptation I Dance Into Your Heart. In the cheaply produced B-Movie, she convinced with her charisma and voice and was acclaimed for the first time in the Motion Picture Herald.

In the following time, Monroe corrected her slight overbite and whitened her teeth. Her new agent Johnny Hyde, the influential vice president of the William Morris Agency, ordered a cartilaginous elevation on the tip of her nose to be removed. This is why Marilyn has a different appearance in the films after 1949.

Hyde managed to get a small guest role conceived for her alongside Groucho Marx in Love Happy, the last film of the Marx Brothers. Marx plays a detective, Monroe, a seductive client. Monroe's brief appearance impressed the producers so much that they sent her to New York for the U.S. advertising campaign and premiere.

While she was on the east coast, she made a well-known series of pin-up photos with André de Dienes on Tobay Beach, Long Island.

After the Love Happy advertising campaign, she was unemployed again and contacted photographer Tom Kelley. In addition to advertising photos, she had herself photographed for a series of professional nude images that would cause a sensation in her later life.

As her popularity grew, Hyde was able to include her in the B-movie A Ticket to Tomahawk in 1950 with a small appearance as a dancer and singer.

Lucille Ryman Carrol, MGM's director for talent, stood up for her with director and Oscar winner John Huston. She then got her first significant role in a vast production in Asphalt Jungle. In three scenes of just five minutes, she shows excellent performance of the naive Angela Finlay, the lover of an older, fraudulent lawyer: a role Marilyn Monroe considered one of her best throughout her life.

In early 1950 she appeared as the Groupie Polly in the Mickey Rooney film Roller Skating Fever.

Other small roles included Dusky Ledoux, a semi-silky model, in the inexpensively produced film The Lone Champion, and Iris Martin, the smart receptionist in a newspaper office, in Hometown Story.

Through Hyde's efforts, she also got a more substantial supporting role, which seemed to be written primarily for her.

In the tragicomedy All about Eve, with Bette Davis in the leading role, she played the ambitious young actress Claudia Caswell.

Shortly before his death, Johnny Hyde had negotiated a seven-year contract with 20th Century Fox, which she signed in October 1950. The deal tied her to the film studio for several years as part of the star system and required her to participate in a certain number of films per year. But now she had a regular income for the first time.

In 1951 she met Michael Tschechow, with whom she took additional private acting lessons.

She attended courses in literature and art at the University of California in Los Angeles.

In the same year, she had small roles in the drama Hometown Story and the comedies As Young as You Feel, Love Nest and Let's Make It Legal. All four movies were produced on a small budget and were moderately successful.

Her screen presence, however, was remarkable, especially in Love Nest as an attractive rival to the leading actress June Haver.

Monroe appeared as a presenter at the 1951 Oscars. She presented the sound Oscar for All about Eve, which won six Oscars.

In March 1952, Monroe provoked a worldwide sex scandal. Already in 1949, she had posed naked for Tom Kelley, however only now one of the nudes was published as a calendar page. The photo shows Monroe naked on red velvet. She justified the gaffe with the remark: "I had to pay my rent! To the question of a journalist: "Did you have nothing on?" she replied: "Yes! The radio!". With her smart answer, she saved the career that had just begun. Financially, the calendar was a complete success. In 1949 she was paid only 50 dollars for the photo session. In December 1953 the photo appeared again in the first issue of Playboy. Until 1956, several calendars published photos from the meeting.

Other film studios became aware of it and began to promote her.

20th Century Fox finally leased her to RKO Pictures for Fritz Lang's environmental study Before the New Day. Beside Barbara Stanwyck, she played a young, self-confident sardine packer in a fish factory. The film's success is partly due to Marilyn Monroe. Despite mixed reviews, the viewers were curious about the provocative actress.

Again with 20th Century Fox, she got her first leading role. In Don't Bother to Knock, she convinced Richard Widmark in the dramatic role of a psychopathic nanny.

But there were no further serious role offers. Her performances were mostly limited to the naive, sexy blonde character.

In the comedy, We Are Not Married; she is named Mrs. Mississippi.

In the turbulent screwball comedy Darling, I Become Younger she acted the teenage secretary of a scientist, played by Cary Grant.

In addition to her beauty, she was praised for her comedic talent. In the same year, an operation on her appendix made hit the headlines and triggered a wave of fan letters.

It was at this time that Monroe received her first awards, including the Photoplay Award, which honored her as the most significant public favorite.

Comedies and music films with international success 1953-1954

In January 1953 Niagara came to the screen. The movie was announced with Marilyn Monroe as the "eighth wonder of the world." She plays a seductive, unscrupulous wife at Joseph Cotten's company who fatally fails with her murder plans. Henry Hathaway staged the thriller in the style of the film noir. Against the theatrical background of Niagara Falls, Hathaway impressively staged Monroe's erotic charisma as a femme fatale. Niagara was the milestone in her career and finally made her an international movie star.

Monroe had already received the role of the diamond loving and burlesque Lorelei Lee in the musical Gentlemen Prefer Blondes on her birthday in 1952, an adaptation of the successful Broadway musical of the same name. Directed by Howard Hawks, the shooting began immediately after the completion of Niagara.

Jane Russell was announced as the biggest star and received ten times Monroe's salary.

The "brightly colored" comedy is primarily fun to watch but contains a few minor side shots to materialism.

Monroe sings Diamonds Are a Girl's Best Friend, one of her most famous songs, in a dance scene. After the great success of the movie, she and her film partner took their hand's and shoe's prints at Grauman's Chinese Theatre in the summer of 1953.

She had a similar role in 1953 under the direction of Jean Negulesco in the film comedy How to Marry a Millionaire, the first Cinemascope film production.

She plays the shortsighted Pola, who is looking for a rich man, alongside Lauren Bacall and Betty Grable.

This film replaces Betty Grable as the most popular pin-up girl of US soldiers. Marilyn Monroe was also the guarantee for the success of 20th Century Fox's new film process, which compared her attractive body to the effect of the anamorphic lens.
In the same year, she had her first appearance on television. In Jack Benny's show, she appeared with a little sketch and a song. She promoted the new cinema experience Cinemascope.

In December 1953 Monroe had signed a contract with the United Service Organizations for a concert tour to war-torn South Korea through Bob Hope. In February 1954 she sang for the soldiers of the allied US armed forces. The short tour was a great success. Despite the icy weather, she performed in a light evening dress, which is why she fell ill with pneumonia after the trip.

In the spring of 1954, River of No Return was premiered, the only classical western in which Monroe played a leading role.

Her film partner was Robert Mitchum; the director was Otto Preminger. During the shooting Monroe hurt her ankle, which delayed the production of the movie. In many scenes of the movie, Monroe can only be seen with covered legs. There were disputes with Preminger. He had said in an interview: "Marilyn Monroe is like Lassie. Monroe commented on the film with the words: "I think I deserve something better than a third-rate cowboy film in which acting is only secondary to the landscape and the Cinemascope method."

The movie There's No Business Like Show Business, made in 1954, is an elaborate production in color and a tribute to the composer Irving Berlin. She plays a dresser who makes a career as a dancer. The role she took over only because the Fox-Studios promised her in return the leading role in Billy Wilders comedy The Seven Year Itch (1955).

From 1953 to 1954, Monroe became the most exceptional financial success of the 20th Century Fox. Unlike her unfavorable seven-year contract with 20th Century Fox in 1950, in 1953 she signed a contract with RCA Records that allowed her to release vocal recordings from the films under her name outside the regular soundtrack.

Acting lessons in New York and more challenging roles 1955-1957

At the end of 1954, Monroe moved to New York. From February 1955 she attended courses at the Actors Studio and learned the Method Acting. The acting teacher Lee Strasberg became her mentor, his wife Paula advised Monroe during the shooting of the following movies.

In the same year, she legally changed her name from Norma Jeane Mortenson to Marilyn Monroe.Already in 1953, there were conflicts with the 20th Century Fox. Monroe insisted on more challenging roles, and she had already rejected several scripts. This led to a compromise in 1954.

For her participation in the movie, There's No Business Like Show Business she had been promised the leading role in the film The Seven Year Itch directed by Billy Wilder.

The comedy already ran successfully as a play on Broadway.

Monroe plays "The Girl," who puts her underwear in the fridge in midsummer. The shooting began in 1955. The film became one of her greatest successes.

The scene in which her dress is blown up over a New York subway tunnel was also made legendary by the photo taken by Sam Shaw.

However, the scene is staged. The draught above the shafts is not enough to blow up a dress.

In another scene of the movie, she parodied a femme fatale to the point of ridicule.

After the end of the shooting, she separated from her longtime acting teacher Natascha Lytess.

Her new acting teacher became Paula Strasberg, the wife of Lee Strasberg.

In the year 1956, a creative and professional turning point became obvious. In December 1954 Monroe had founded her own company, Marilyn Monroe Productions Inc., together with the photographer Milton Greene. Monroe held 51% of the shares, Greene 49%.

At the time, Monroe was Hollywood's third contracted female actress, along with Mary Pickford and Ida Lupino, to set up her own production company. This led to a scandal in Hollywood, especially as her company had sued 20th Century Fox for violating the contract. Despite repeated reminders from Monroe, 20th Century Fox had not fulfilled its obligations under the seven-year contract from 1950 and had not repaid her work for the film The Seven Years' Darned. A settlement was reached. Finally, Marilyn Monroe received her payment afterward. The seven-year contract was terminated. By mutual agreement, both parties agreed to work out a new deal.

In the same year, Marilyn Monroe stood again in front of the camera in Hollywood. The film Bus Stop was made under new contractual conditions. Monroe now had a say in the selection of the script and the director. This modern western drama had celebrated successes on Broadway before. The director Joshua Logan was engaged for the new film. Logan also had experience with Method Acting, which convinced Monroe.

Especially for this role, she acquired a southern accent. The critics celebrated her acting performance right after the premiere. Nevertheless, commercial success did not materialize, especially in Europe.

In England, she stood in front of the camera in the romance The Prince and the Showgirl in 1957. Her partner was the classical actor Sir Laurence Olivier who also directed the film. This film is the only work by Marilyn Monroe Productions Inc. in collaboration with Milton Greene. During the shooting, there were tensions between Olivier and Monroe. Despite some awards, the film did not bring the expected success in the United States.

Most Successful Comedy and character role 1958-1962

After Monroe hadn't made a film for two years, she appeared in August 1958 alongside Tony Curtis and Jack Lemmon in Billy Wilders movie comedy Some Like It Hot.

She played "Sugar Kane," the singer and ukulele player in a women's band.

In the film, she was to sing several songs, including I Want to Be Loved by You.

The shooting was difficult. Monroe interrupted the scenes countless times because she was not satisfied with herself. Often she appeared on the set without having learned her lyrics; sometimes, she came hours late. Afraid of not playing well, the pill-addicted actress could only sleep with high doses of barbiturates, she also drank too much.

Her acting coach Paula Strasberg, under whose influence she was, and her husband Arthur Miller often clashed with Wilder. This not only made the shooting more challenging but also extended it by 20 days and pushed up production costs.

Some like it hot became the greatest success of both Wilder and Monroe and was one of the box office hits of 1959. The film is a classic today and is considered the best comedy of all time.

To fulfill her contract with 20th Century Fox, in 1960 Monroe played alongside Yves Montand in George Cukor's Let's Make. Despite funny plots and good reviews, the movie was not a commercial success.

Her last completed film was John Huston's Misfits in 1961. This movie marked a long-awaited change into character. The film was wholly dedicated to the criticism of the American cowboys' dream of freedom. In the United States Misfits was called a European movie, and because of its depressive atmosphere, it was a failure.

The role of Roslyn had been written primarily for Monroe by the screenwriter Arthur Miller. However, Monroe herself found the role too close to her person.

In her last, unfinished film Something's Got to Give, she was supposed to act in serious, modern clothes that were in keeping with the taste of the times. The movie was again a light comedy. The shooting dragged on endlessly as she hardly appeared on the stage due to illness. Before she started shooting she flew to New York to work on the role with Lee Strasberg in the Actors Studio. When the first day of shooting was on April 23, 1962, she got notified that she was ill through producer Henry T. Weinstein. She had contracted a virus infection on her trip to New York. In total, she appeared only on 17 of 30 shooting days. Due to her absence because of illness, the shooting costs increased disproportionately, which also burdened the Fox-Studios because, at the same time, the costs of shooting Cleopatra turned into a catastrophe.

During the shooting, Monroe made her last public appearance at the birthday party of US President John F. Kennedy at Madison Square Garden when she sang Happy Birthday, Mr. President, in a skin-colored dress designed by Jean Louis. This performance was against the will of the Fox Studios. He eventually got Monroe fired because she was on sick leave and still flew to the presidential gala in New York. Later, after negotiations with the studios, work was to continue on Something's Got to Give. But the movie couldn't be finished because Monroe died before that.

Monroe had one of her last major appearances on film footage that would enter the history of photography with Bert Stern's photo series The Last Session, which he made alone with Monroe as a model in a hotel room shortly before her death. In the three-day photo session for the American magazine Vogue, the actress appeared relaxed and comprehensive in front of the camera.

According to Stern, some of the best shots were taken when Monroe was already drunk. On some of the unauthorized photos, the scar of a gallbladder operation can be clearly seen, "the consequences of which had turned the curvy sex bomb into a slender and fragile-looking woman in her last year of life" She censored or destroyed some of the snapshots that made her appear unfavorable by applying a large "X" to the diapositives with nail polish or scratching them with hairpins.

Stern later also used the photographs censored by Monroe in his book.

In some biographies, the book was referred to as Marilyn Monroe's Swan Song.

After The Last Session, however, Monroe did more photoshoots, so that Bert Stern's book title only contributed to the formation of legends.

However, because Stern published almost all of the material, the series remains the most extensively documented photo session with her.

Private Life

On June 19, 1942, 16-year-old Norma Jeane married James Dougherty, a neighbor five years his senior. Both mothers had arranged the young couple's marriage to save Norma from another stay in the orphanage. "Jim" worked at Lockheed Aircraft. Through him, she met Robert Mitchum, one of Jim's colleagues.

Mitchum was to become her later film partner in River of No Return. Dougherty was conscripted into the Navy shortly after the wedding. Meanwhile, Norma Jeane was discovered as a model by the army photographer David Conover and started her career as Marilyn Monroe. On September 13, 1946, both divorced by mutual consent.

The Catholic marriage with the baseball star Joe DiMaggio was celebrated on January 14, 1954, and lasted only nine months.

In 1952 Monroe met DiMaggio at an arranged blind date during the shooting of the movie Darling, I'm getting younger. She later said she didn't want to meet him at all.

She imagined he was wearing brightly colored ties and had muscles like a bodybuilder. The marriage was followed intensively by the public and the tabloid press.

DiMaggio, who had retired from active baseball, wanted a housewife while Monroe was at the height of her career. DiMaggio used to reply bitterly that when his wife told him how she had been admired once again, he remembered that feeling well. He could not bear that his career was over and his wife had so much admiration.

DiMaggio spent a lot of time in front of the TV, which bored Monroe again. During the shooting of the movie The Seven Years, Monroe's dress was blown up over a subway shaft in one scene, DiMaggio had a jealousy attack in front of hundreds of viewers. Their marriage suffered from both opposites and was divorced on October 31, 1954, because of mutual cruelty. In the spring of 1961, however, Monroe and DiMaggio began to maintain friendly contact again. After Monroe's death, DiMaggio brought red roses to her burial chamber three times a week over 20 years. In 1982 this permanent order was terminated without reason.

Monroe and the famous playwright Arthur Miller got married on June 29, 1956.

For him, she converted to Judaism.

The two had met in 1951 during the shooting of the movie As Young as You Feel by Elia Kazan.

Monroe saw in Miller a defender and father replacement. Finally, she had a family where she could take care of Miller's children from his first marriage. Both were happy; Miller's love gave her security and recognition.

They also wanted to have children together. For him, Monroe could imagine being only a housewife.

When Miller was accused of sympathizing with the Communists in 1957, Monroe stood by her husband.

The marriage, however, was overshadowed by three spontaneous miscarriages caused by Monroe's endometriosis.

Miller wrote the script for the movie Misfits especially for her. But the problematic shooting marked the end of the marriage.

Miller became desperate for her considerable consumption of tablets.

Monroe, on the other hand, had read his diary, in which he described her, among other things, as an unpredictable and helpless infant woman, for whom he felt only compassion.

After numerous marital disputes, the couple divorced on January 20, 1961, without any mutual claims.

Last years of life

The art figure Marilyn Monroe, also known as MM, already became a legend in the 1950s.

The difference between the natural beauty of the young Norma Jeane with brunette curls and the perfect blonde sex symbol Marilyn Monroe with a staged image including the attributes make-up, facial expressions, voice and body style became apparent in 1952.

Marilyn Monroe regarded herself as a committed actress. She hated the limitation of her person to the "stupid blonde."

From the middle of the 1950's she tried to find more serious roles. Because of her image, she had problems with the aging.

During her last seven years, she was always in medical and psychoanalytic treatment. The divorce of Arthur Miller after the end of the shooting of Misfits and the death of Clark Gables worsened her suffering.

In 1962 she visited her psychoanalyst twice a day. Towards the end of her life, she tried to fight her manic depression and the resulting self-doubt more and more with psychotropic drugs; she also drank too much alcohol.

Today, some experts consider Marilyn Monroe, a victim of psychoanalysis.

Death, burial

Monroe died in the night between August 4 and August 5, 1962, at the age of 36 in her bed at 12305 Fifth Helena Drive, Brentwood, Los Angeles. A judicially ordered autopsy established the cause of death on August 5, 1962. According to autopsy reports by pathologist Thomas Noguchi, the cause of death was an overdose of the barbiturate Nembutal in combination with the sleeping pill chloral hydrate. The autopsy of the body revealed that the dead woman was healthy according to her age. Her death certificate says "a probable suicide." An accidental overdose is also possible. Many theories of murder have also been circulating since then.

Monroe was buried on August 8, 1962, in a bronze coffin in the Corridor of Memories in the Westwood Village Memorial Park Cemetery in Los Angeles. The funeral was organized by the former husband Joe DiMaggio, the half-sister Berniece Inez Miracle, née Baker, and her private secretary. The ecumenical funeral took place in the closest family and circle of friends. Lee Strasberg delivered the funeral speech written by Carl Sandburg, and the Reverend of the Village Church of Westwood preached about the 23rd Psalm.

Suspicions of the cause of death

There are several suspicions about Monroe's cause of death. The most popular conspiracy theory about her death is that President John F. Kennedy had her murdered by the CIA because his affair with Marilyn Monroe was a danger to his office. The barbiturate Nembutal could have been administered via an enemy. In this case, the chloral hydrate must have been taken orally with a drink she had made with an unknown visitor arriving at 10 pm. This drink could have served as a narcotic. An affair between Justice Minister Robert F. Kennedy and Monroe was virtually ruled out in the 1990s. Monroe never spoke about an affair in interviews. What is certain is that John F. Kennedy's brother Robert, together with his brother-in-law Peter Lawford, had visited the actress on the night of her death and the day before under unexplained circumstances.

Moreover, according to police reports, many phone calls came and went from Monroe's house on the night of her death. The thesis that the Kennedys were responsible for Monroe's death was first put forward in a BBC documentary in 1986. However, there is no documented, confirmed evidence of this theory. Some pieces of evidence have been lost.

According to another version, the Mafia was responsible for Monroe's death. She had murdered the star and left traces in the direction of the Kennedy brothers to block their action against organized crime. Magistrates stopped attempts by investigators to reopen the case in 1981, 1985 and 1992 because there was no severe doubt of suicide.

Biographer Donald Spoto speculated that Monroe's death was the result of a gross medical error. Her psychiatrist Ralph R. Greenson gave his patient her enema with chloral hydrate against sleep disorders. At this time, however, Monroe is said to have already taken a barbiturate according to a prescription from the doctor Hyman Engelberg. Earlier, Engelberg was commissioned by Greenson to take over Monroe's medication. On the evening of August 4, 1962, Greenson then administered the enema with chloral hydrate, which caused Monroe's death with the barbiturate he had previously taken, without consulting Engelberg beforehand.

The ZDF television documentary Mordfall Marilyn? From May 2015 suggests that Monroe had an affair with Greenson. She died from an injection Greenson injected into her chest on the night of her death.

What speaks against suicide theory above all is the fact that Monroe was under contract with the production company Fox and was due to work the following Monday. That both Life and Paris-Match showed her on the title that the last films were box-office successes and that she had written about the happiest time of her life one day before her death.

Legacy

Monroe's wealth at the time of her death was about a million dollars.

Her rights are owned by "Marilyn Monroe LLC," a company founded in 1999. A commissioned agency manages the copyright concerning the image of the actress. This includes her appearance, name, signature, and voice. The copyright for photos, songs, and movies is not included. The agency markets Monroe in advertising and the fashion industry or for general products such as costume jewelry, dolls, calendars, posters, postcards, bed linen or ashtrays. However, these rights have no legal significance concerning freedom of the press and the fine arts.

This situation was caused by Monroe's testament from 1961, which was partly written without skill. As early as 1962, Monroe wanted to change her will because she had separated from her former psychoanalyst. Monroe had considered the doctor in her will. The "Marilyn Monroe LLC" is wholly owned by Anna Strasberg, Lee Strasberg's third wife. After deduction of the entire private property and still existing business shares had been awarded to him by the will. This happened only after the death of Monroe's mother on March 11, 1984. Lee Strasberg had already died on February 17, 1982. Since Lee Strasberg had disinherited his remaining family, the entire remaining assets were bequeathed to his widow.

The company "Marilyn Monroe LLC" is controversial and has been prosecuted several times. Complaints were settled by settlement. Different legislations in the states of the United States obstruct a generally valid legal basis. Although the company is also registered in different countries, there is no legal force for the international market. Marilyn Monroe LLC" currently has an annual revenue of approximately 2.5 million dollars.

Films and Performances

From 1947 to 1962 Marilyn Monroe took part in 30 movies, plus some special appearances. She starred in a B-movie and 13 big productions. Apart from a leading role in the B-movie Ladies of the Chorus (1948) and a much-acclaimed short appearance in the comedy Love Happy (1949), she had only minor roles in the beginning, often as an attractive secretary. In the movie Film noir The Asphalt Jungle (1950) she could show her acting talent for the first time, she had another essential supporting role in All About Eve (1950). Her screen presence was also remarkable in small roles. In Don't Bother to Knock (1952) she could convince in the leading role as a psychopathic nanny.

With the thriller Niagara (1953), which impressively staged her erotic charisma as a femme fatale, she became a film star.

In classics like Gentlemen Prefer Blondes (1953) and How to Marry a Millionaire (1953) persuaded her in her typical role as a naive, sensual blonde with her talent as a comedian and singer and advanced her to the most excellent star of Hollywood. It was followed by the Western River of No Return (1954) and the film musical There's No Business Like Show Business (1954).

In the comedy The Seven Year Itch1955) by Billy Wilder, she had a brilliant role. For her character portrayal in Bus Stop (1956) and her performance in The Prince and the Showgirl (1957), she got good reviews.
She had her greatest success with the wild comedy Some Like It Hot (1959). Let's Make Love (1960) failed to bring the hoped-for success despite good reviews. The Misfits (1961) she made the longed-for change into character. Something's Got to Give (1962) remained unfinished because Marilyn Monroe died before the end of the shooting.

Marilyn Monroe's regular German dubbing voice was Margot Leonard.

She appeared in 1953 with a little sketch as well as the song Bye Bye Baby in the TV show of Jack Benny and promoted the new cinema experience Cinemascope.

In 1955 she gave together with Milton and Amy Greene a live interview with the journalist Edward R. Murrow for his show Person to Person at their estate in West-Connecticut.

In the documentary USO - Wherever They Go! about the United Service Organizations, a half-minute recording of their appearance before the soldiers of the 3rd US Infantry Division in South Korea in 1954 was recorded and commented on.

Recordings of her performance at the 1962 birthday party in honor of President John F. Kennedy at Madison Square Garden were later shown on television.

Marilyn Monroe also appeared as a singer in many of her movies. Her most famous songs are Diamonds Are a Girl's Best Friend, and you Wanna love me.

There's No Business Like Show Business became the evergreen.

Her concert tour for the soldiers of the 3rd US Infantry Division in South Korea in 1954 found overwhelming resonance.

Monroe also recorded some of her songs on vinyl, but she never acted as a professional singer.

At the beginning of her career, Marilyn Monroe was awarded the Photoplay Award for her popularity and public image.

She has twice received the Henrietta Award as the world's most popular actress at the Golden Globe Awards.

Her most prestigious film awards include a nomination for the British Film Academy Award (BAFTA) for The Darned Year, a Golden Globe nomination for Bus Stop and a David di Donatello, an Étoile de Cristal and BAFTA and Laurel nominations for The Prince and the Dancer.

For Some Like It Hot, she won the Golden Globe in the Best Actress in Comedy or Musical category and ranked second at the Laurel Awards.

Five times she was nominated for the Laurel Award as the most prominent female star.

In 1953, she left her hand and footprints at Grauman's Chinese Theatre with Jane Russell.

She was honored with a star on the Hollywood Walk of Fame in 1960.

Reception in art and culture

Already during his lifetime, Monroe had the status of a world star; film studios introduced actresses like Diana Dors, Jayne Mansfield or Mamie van Doren to the screen as her competition.

The American Film Institute ranked her 6th among the 25 biggest female American film stars.

Many famous artists like Salvador Dalí or Andy Warhol used Monroe in their paintings, such as Warhol's Marilyn Diptych or James Gill's Pink Marilyn.

Numerous musicians also wrote songs about her. A well-known example is Elton Johns Candle in the Wind. Rock bands like Marilyn Manson or Norma Jean use Monroe's name.

She loved eye-catching dresses that were as skin-tight as possible and were supposed to show off her body in the best possible way, even though she liked to wear T-shirts and shorts in her private life.

Her reputation was that she did not wear underwear, to which she also gladly referred journalists.

Marilyn Monroe can be described as one of the most outstanding female cult figures in history, whose look was copied by artists such as Madonna, Kylie Minogue, Anna Nicole Smith, Gwen Stefani or Christina Aguilera.

Her hairstyle with shoulder-length blond hair falling into soft curls still has icon status today. At the start of her film career in each movie, she had a different blonde tone.

In the field of decorative cosmetics, she was an excellent make-up artist on her account and is still a widely copied archetype. Typical for her was the veiled look, that she created by false eyelashes in the corner of her eye and elaborate eyeliner drawing, the slightly open, sensual mouth, which she applied with up to five different shades of lipstick and make-up line for shine, and her painted beauty spot. It took her up to three hours a day to create herself as perfect. If something failed, she started the procedure all over again.

The first issue of Playboy contained the legendary nude photos of Tom Kelley and thus established the basis of the Playboy calendar sheet. In 2012, the 50th anniversary of Monroe's death, the magazine honored her posthumously as Hugh Hefner's favorite playmate in a special edition of the December issue.

Ray Anthony composed the song My Marilyn and sang it for Monroe in 1952 on the occasion of a promotion for the film Niagara.

The song Marilyn Monroe by Andre Heller appeared in 1972.

In 1973 the song Candle in the Wind appeared on Elton John's album Goodbye Yellow Brick Road as a tribute to Monroe. The song was re-released in 1997 for the funeral of Princess Diana with modified lyrics.

In 1974 Hildegard Knef released a song called, And Her Name Was Marilyn.

In 1975 Cliff Jones wrote the musical Hey Marilyn about the life of Marilyn Monroe, starring Beverly D'Angelo.

Udo Lindenberg sang a German version of Candle in the Wind on his 1979 album Der Detektiv - Rock Revue II. Title of the song is Goodbye, Norma Jean.

In 1981 the horror punk band Misfits wrote the song Who Killed Marilyn. The name of the band was derived from Monroe's film The Misfits.

In 1994 the band Suede wrote a homage to Monroe with the song Heroine on their album Dog Man Star album.

Marilyn Monroe is mentioned in many songs, among others in Madonna's Vogue, Billy Joel's We Didn't Start the Fire, Dance in the Dark by Lady Gaga.